KU-250-317

DOG
PERSONALITIES

DOG
PERSONALITIES

Jono Yates

BANTAM PRESS

LONDON · TORONTO · SYDNEY · AUCKLAND · JOHANNESBURG

TRANSWORLD PUBLISHERS
61–63 Uxbridge Road, London W5 5SA
www.penguin.co.uk

Transworld is part of the Penguin Random House group of companies
whose addresses can be found at global.penguinrandomhouse.com

First published in Great Britain in 2018 by Bantam Press
an imprint of Transworld Publishers

Copyright © Jono Yates 2018

Jono Yates has asserted his right under the Copyright,
Designs and Patents Act 1988 to be identified as the author of this work.

A CIP catalogue record for this book
is available from the British Library.

ISBN 9780593080382

Typeset in Din Schrft Neuzeit Grotesk/12pt by www.envyltd.co.uk

Penguin Random House is committed to a sustainable
future for our business, our readers and our planet. This book
is made from Forest Stewardship Council® certified paper.

1 3 5 7 9 10 8 6 4 2

George, 40

In the middle of Dry January. Just
realizing how boring his friends are
without alcohol and reconsidering
his entire social circle.

Ethel, 78

Won't stop waving until you're out
of sight. Never eat before visiting because
she'll get the biscuits out even if you're
absolutely stuffed.

Tony, 24

Just watched his team get absolutely
battered. And then his girlfriend comes
out with 'Cheer up. It's only a game.'

Carly, 20

Was meant to be at her friend's
house party fifteen minutes ago.
She's been sat in her towel for an hour
now and is showing no signs of
going anywhere soon. Sent an
'On my way' text.

Brian, 40

Father of two. Has a pair of Crocs because they're practical. Gets the waiter's attention in a restaurant by drawing in the air with an imaginary pen when he wants to pay. Drives ten miles extra to this petrol station just for the Nectar points.

Sarah, 25

Just had her hair cut for the first time in a year. She hates it but lied to the hairdresser because she's too nice. She's going to go home and cry into a tub of ice cream instead.

Clint, 45

Voted for Trump because he
offered something different.
Now deeply regrets it and fears
nuclear war.

Corporal Grice, 61

Won't stop telling his grandchildren
stories about the war. Their mother
thinks it's inappropriate. He says,
'They have to learn one day, Carol.'

Sandra, 48

Gets into arguments about *Daily Mail* articles on Facebook. Doesn't approve of her daughter's new haircut. At all.

Ollie, 18

Just asked his mum if they could order pizza tonight. She responded with 'Yeah, there's one in the freezer.'

Tim, 30

Has absolutely no Irish heritage
but on 17 March he'll be downing pints
of Guinness and celebrating
St Paddy's Day like he's lived in Dublin
his whole life. Also a regular at Burns
Night shindigs.

Tammy, 25

Woke up feeling old and fat. Going through Facebook photos from five years ago is doing absolutely nothing to help her mood.

Eric, 35

Knocks and waits half a second
before posting a 'Sorry we missed
you' note through the door. Also enjoys
an 'Insufficient postage' sticker.
Bit of a bastard.

Brad, 32

Addicted to Tinder. Carries beard
oil and a comb wherever he goes.
Didn't get the memo about topknots
going out of fashion.

Lily, 25

Works part-time in a Turkish belly-dancing club to pay off her student loan. Her hips don't lie but neither does her bank account.

Omar, 22

Locked himself out of the house again.
Thinks it's time to stop drinking during
the day.

Andy, 24

Saw that you read his message an
hour ago but haven't replied. Already
bitching about you in all his other
group chats.

King, 19

Lies to girls about how much he earns
at his part-time supermarket job. Has 800
followers on Instagram and has added
'Influencer' to his bio.

Geoffrey, 70

Has a Sky Sports account just to watch
the cricket. Carries a packet of Werther's
Originals on him at all times.

Tess, 24

Just checked her boyfriend's Instagram and saw that he liked hundreds of other girls' selfies. Waiting for the perfect time to bring it up.

44

Henrick, 32

Takes vintage fashion a bit too far.
Bought a penny-farthing to ride to work
and is always getting beeped at.

Paddy, 27

Can't stand lager. Bores anyone who will listen with rants about the nutritional value of Guinness and whiskey. Might have a problem.

COUNTRY LIFE

OCTOBER 3 2007

Country sports

Hooray, dog days are back

Lynn, 40

Farmer's wife. Stopped reading women's magazines because they're full of dysfunctional relationships. But these guys look wholesome and happy. These guys give her hope.

Curtis, 25

Still lives with his mum and dad
but flexes for Instagram. Poses with
cars, watches and bottles of vodka
that do not belong to him.

Creg, 28

Played a bit of online poker and
now trying his luck at the real thing.
Just went all in on a 7 and a 2. He'll
be spending the rest of the night
at the bar.

Jim, 20

Hypochondriac. Suffering from
man flu. Far too ill to get up and make
a cup of tea for everyone, despite
having made one for himself twenty
minutes ago.

Tash, 21

Started her dissertation at 9 p.m. the day before the deadline. Now it's 3 a.m. and all she's done is refresh her timeline and get angry at Farmville invites.

Cody, 22

Student, falling behind in class.
Heard Stormzy for the first time last
week. Now dresses like he was born
and raised in South London. He's
from Buckinghamshire.

Mike, 45

Career burglar. Just been caught
attempting a break-in and is now
concealing his anti-vandal-paint-covered
back. 'This bag? No, Officer, never
seen it before in my life.'

Rory, 17

A bit of a rebel. Just got in from a party he snuck out to. Swears he's not been anywhere, despite overwhelming evidence to the contrary.

Scott, 20

Unemployed. Hasn't listened to
anything except Oasis in two years.
Went out last night and still on it.
Has a 'Live Forever' tattoo.

Dianne, 31

Shopped at Aldi before it was cool.
Complains about how busy it is but
will never go anywhere else. Her house
is full of items from the mad aisle in
the middle.

Brandon, 32

Passionate about fishing. Claims to
have caught a 30lb trout in his prime but
has absolutely no evidence to support
that claim. In fact, nobody has seen him
with so much as a goldfish.

Kyle, 28

Was looking forward to going out with friends tonight after a long week. Half an hour into the pre-drinks and he's already overdone it. There's always next week.

Mallek, 34

Car salesman. Would screw over his
mother to make a sale. In the middle
of convincing a single mother that
she needs a car that will go 0–60 in six
seconds. She doesn't.

Sammy, 14

Spends twenty hours a day on Fortnite.
His mum is worried about his studies
but he's far too busy relaxing in
Pleasure Park to care.

Dan, 15

Decided it would be a good idea
to talk back to his teacher. Now
he's stuck in detention while all his
mates play football on the field.
He's consumed with regret.

Yannick, 27

Recently quit caffeine in favour of organic substitutes. Claims that green tea has changed his life. Has written seventeen Facebook statuses about it so far and counting.

Doug, 25

Suffering after too much tequila last
night. Ordered a Bloody Mary and a gin
& tonic to tackle the hangover. It's not
quite worked yet.

Alfie, 11

Nervous about his first day at school but putting on a brave face. Spent an hour in the mirror failing to do his tie before giving up and asking his mum to do it. Things can only get better.

Jess, 24

Just overheard her flatmate saying she's about to go on a McDonald's run. A 2/10 day is turning into a 10/10 day.

Nick, 28

Woke up this morning and decided
to stay in bed all day. Politely asked
his girlfriend to cook breakfast.
She declined.

Tommy, 25

Loves nothing more than barbecued food. Takes great pride in his signature ribs. However, he has a horrible feeling that the last chicken wing wasn't quite done.

Sergeant Claymore, 71

US veteran. Loves his country more
than his family.

Craig, 28

Drinks eight cans of Strongbow Dark
Fruit and then balances them on his
head – every time without fail. Loves the
Arctic Monkeys.

Arthur, 41

Member of the Puggy Blinders.
They run Birmingham. A loyal servant
to his brother Tommy.

Ben, 28

Electrician and FIFA addict.
Believes England were unlucky not
to win the World Cup despite
struggling against teams made up
of cattle farmers.

Hannah, 24

Has an expensive shoe collection but walks barefoot. Has a 'Live, Love, Laugh' sign in her room. Sells daisy chains on Depop.

Bill, 68

Shouts at local children to slow
down when they ride past his house on
their bikes. If you kick your ball into his
garden, don't expect it back.

Lisa, 25

Not quite summer-body-ready
despite her best efforts. Loves
takeaway food.

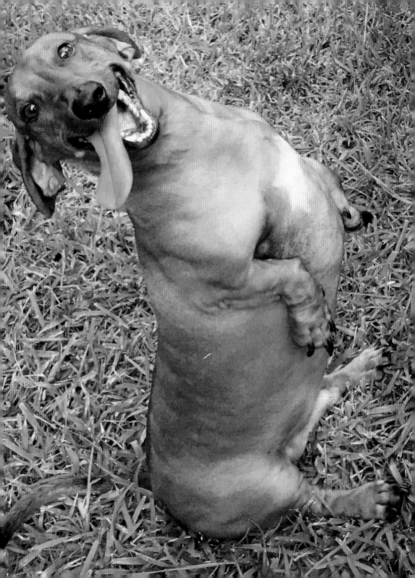

Ken, 40

Retired early. Spends most days
sitting outside, drinking cocktails from
10 a.m. and cooking meat for nobody
but himself. If there's a barbecue,
he's there.

Toby, 26

Left his phone unlocked.
His girlfriend is not happy about the
texts from two years ago asking his
sister's best mate for a lift.

Kylie, 24

Militant member of Greenpeace.
Has been camped on this digger for
a fortnight to save the trees in her
local forest.

Elijah, 20

Discovered grime six months ago.
Now has a completely different dialect
and his teachers are worried.

Dale, 32

Drinks craft beer exclusively. Blends
his own coffee. Pretends to like
foreign cinema but his favourite film is
Transformers.

Tina, 28

Wants to find a nice man to settle down with, but her obsession with Zac Efron is so extreme that no other man will ever take his place. This is a problem.

Gemma, 32

Came to the countryside for a weekend
to get away from city life. Now she's
considering getting divorced, quitting
her job, buying a caravan and staying.

Matty, 32

Eats Greggs for breakfast every day.
Doesn't understand why wolf-whistling
at girls is now frowned upon. Drinks
four cans of Carling every night.

120

Dorothy, 83

Completes ten crosswords a day.
Believes everything she reads in the
newspaper and starts every other
sentence with 'Kids these days . . .'

Herman, 45

Entrepreneur and visionary in his field.
Enjoys driving around the countryside in
his Mercedes so that everyone knows
he's rich.

PICTURE ACKNOWLEDGEMENTS

Every effort has been made to obtain the necessary permissions with reference to copyright material. We apologize for any omissions in this respect and will be pleased to make the appropriate acknowledgements in future editions.

The author would like to thank

Lia Silver (page 5), George Kirkham (page 6), Lee Dearden (page 9), @muggsyboguestthebulldog (page 10), Lee Storey (page 13), @captain_jacksonn (page 14), Stacey Robins (page 17), Emily Plunkett (page 18), Dee Brunt (page 20), Sharon Harrison (page 22), @jugcalledisaac (page 25), Abby Bebbink (page 27), Isabel Pardo (page 29), @brucebullterrierking (page 31), @hipster_doodle (page 33), Bonnie Dunne (page 34), Danielle Puma (page 37), James Cooper (page 38), Hailey Edy (page 40), Jay Hambleton (page 42), Joanna Cintora (page 45), Jessica Bell (page 46 and 52), Claire Blackwell (page 49), Julie Pegler (page 50), Jason Craigen (page 54), Dan McCarthy (page 57), Karen Buckley (page 58), @rocksthehusky (page 61 and 72), Cara Michelle Stirton (page 62), Ellie Foster (page 65), Jacs Louise (page 66), Kate Battams (page 69), Katherine Lilley (page 70), Lauren McLean (page 74), Liam Redmond (page 77), Livvy Brewer (page 78), Lyndsey Cook (page 81), Mairead Hughes (page 82), @fritztheshiba (page 85), Michelle Bogue (page 86), Nicola Griffin (page 89), Paulina Pobiegly (page 90), Raina Melville (page 92), Robert Conner (page 94), Samantha French (page 97), Samantha Jawook (page 98), Sarah Dart (page 101 and 126, top right), Natasha Boatwright (page 102), Sarah Rodriguez Robertson (page 105), @orangedogfallon (page 106), Shaun Hornsby (page 109), Spencer Baker (page 110), Stephanie Smith (page 113), Tom Marsh (page 114), Toyah Thubron (page 117), Nikki Sage (page 118), Willem Arnhem (page 121), Patsy Baldock (page 122), Simon David Botha (page 125), Jenna Rowley (page 126, top left), Stephanie Dassinger (page 126, bottom left), Dan Loveless (page 126, bottom right) and Andrew Michael Johnston (page 128).